D1126228

SOURCES OF LIGHT

Simon Rose

MEDIA ENHANCED BOOKS

AV²
BY WEIGL™

ADDED VALUE • AUDIO VISUAL

www.av2books.com

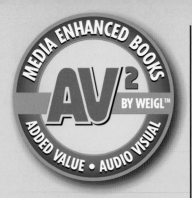

AV² provides enriched content that supplements and complements this book. Weigl's AV² books strive to create inspired learning and engage young minds in a total learning experience.

Your AV² Media Enhanced books come alive with...

Audio
Listen to sections of the book read aloud.

Key Words
Study vocabulary, and complete a matching word activity.

Go to **www.av2books.com,** and enter this book's unique code.

Video
Watch informative video clips.

Quizzes
Test your knowledge.

BOOK CODE

P 9 2 7 3 6 2

Embedded Weblinks
Gain additional information for research.

Slide Show
View images and captions, and prepare a presentation.

AV² by Weigl brings you media enhanced books that support active learning.

Try This!
Complete activities and hands-on experiments.

... and much, much more!

Published by AV² by Weigl
350 5th Avenue, 59th Floor
New York, NY 10118
Website: www.av2books.com   www.weigl.com

Library of Congress Cataloging-in-Publication Data

Rose, Simon, 1961-
 Sources of light / Simon Rose.
    p. cm. -- (Light science)
Includes index.
 ISBN 978-1-61690-836-2 (hardcover : alk. paper) -- ISBN 978-1-61690-840-9 (softcover : alk. paper) -- ISBN 978-1-61690-386-2 (online)
 1. Light--Juvenile literature. I. Title.
 QC360.R66 2012
 535'.35--dc22
                        2011014125

Printed in the United States of America in North Mankato, Minnesota
1 2 3 4 5 6 7 8 9 0 15 14 13 12 11

052011
WEP290411

Senior Editor: Heather Kissock   Art Director: Terry Paulhus

Every reasonable effort has been made to trace ownership and to obtain permission to reprint copyright material. The publishers would be pleased to have any errors or omissions brought to their attention so that they may be corrected in subsequent printings.

Weigl acknowledges Getty Images as its primary image supplier for this title.

CONTENTS

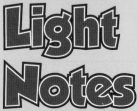

Light Notes

The first torches were created more than 70,000 years ago. At that time, people would soak moss in animal fat. The moss would then be put in a shell or a hollow rock and set on fire. People used these torches to see in darkness.

Studying Light

Light comes in many forms. Flip a light switch, and light fills the room. Walk outside, and the Sun lights up the neighborhood. People rely on both **natural** and **artificial** light to help them see the world they live in.

Human eyes need light in order to see. All light comes from a light source. A light source is any object that produces or **reflects** light. If an object is not a source of light, light must shine on the object before it can be seen.

Thousands of years ago, people depended on the Sun and fire as their main sources of light. When the Sun set at night, people would have used something as simple as a burning stick to light their way. Later, candles were created to make light.

Today, most people live in homes that have electric lights. Most of these lights are in the form of light bulbs. Light bulbs are much safer to use inside a building than a candle or torch.

▄▄ Flipping a light switch on generates electricity. This is how much of today's artificial light is made.

Natural and Artificial Light

Light comes from many sources. Some sources of light are created by humans. Others occur on their own in nature. There are three broad categories that cover sources of natural light.

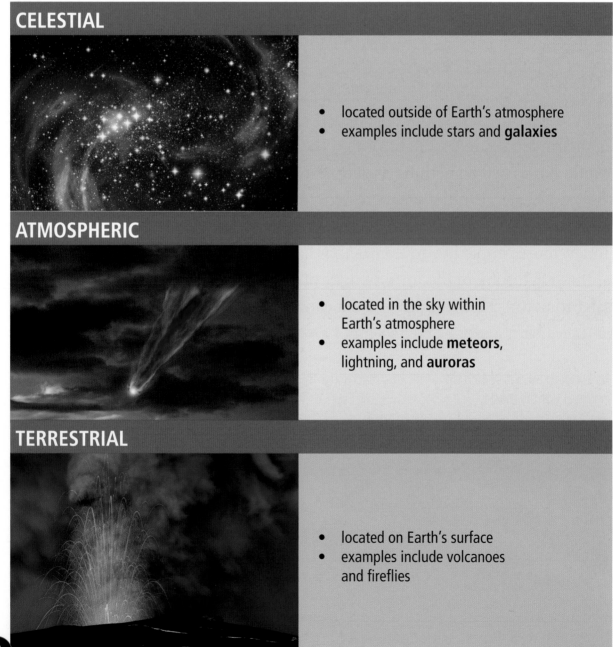

CELESTIAL

- located outside of Earth's atmosphere
- examples include stars and **galaxies**

ATMOSPHERIC

- located in the sky within Earth's atmosphere
- examples include **meteors**, lightning, and **auroras**

TERRESTRIAL

- located on Earth's surface
- examples include volcanoes and fireflies

Artificial light sources are those that humans have developed to help them see when natural light is not available. There are three main types of artificial light.

CHEMICAL

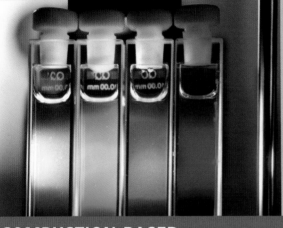

- mixing **chemical compounds** to produce energy that can be converted into light
- examples include light sticks and **fluorescent** dyes

COMBUSTION-BASED

- burning to produce heat, which then creates light
- examples include candles, lanterns, and torches

ELECTRIC

- converting other sources of energy, such as coal, wind, or water, into electric power
- examples include light bulbs and **halogen** lamps

The Sun

Most of the natural light on Earth comes from the Sun. The Sun is an enormous ball of hot gases. Hydrogen is the main gas that forms the Sun. The temperature of the Sun's surface is about 10,000° Fahrenheit (5,538° Celsius).

The Sun uses **nuclear energy** to produce light and heat. The extreme heat and pressure found on the Sun cause hydrogen atoms to **fuse** together. This fusion creates a new gas called helium. The process of making the new gas causes the Sun to constantly glow. The glowing light travels all the way to Earth, 93 million miles (150 million kilometers) away.

Sunlight travels at about 186,282 miles (299,792 km) per second. It takes about 8 minutes for the light from the Sun to reach Earth.

Earth is constantly rotating. Sunlight is always shining on Earth, but it only reaches the side that is facing the Sun. This gives Earth its night and day cycle.

The Sun converts 700 million tons (635 million tonnes) of its hydrogen **atoms** into helium atoms every second. Over time, the Sun will use up its supply of hydrogen. However, due to the Sun's size, it will take a long time for this to happen. Scientists believe the Sun has enough hydrogen to remain active for about another 5 billion years.

The extreme heat and pressure found on the Sun sometimes causes solar flares. These massive eruptions of gas can lead to power outages on Earth.

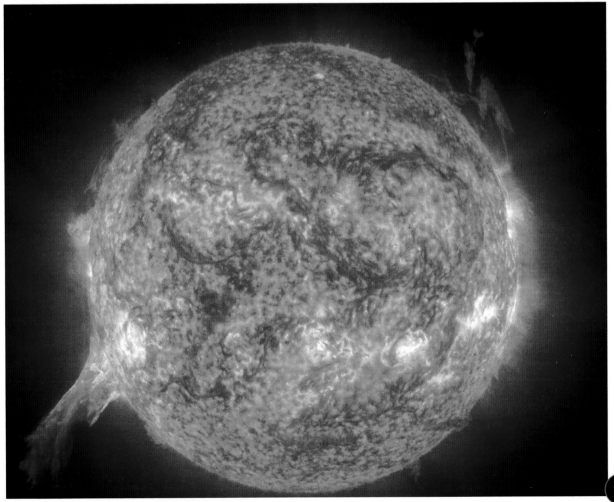

Lights in the Sky

The Sun is one of many stars in the sky. It appears brighter than other stars because it is closer to Earth. At night, however, part of Earth faces away from the Sun. It then receives some light from the other stars in the sky. These stars create light much like the Sun.

Other objects in the sky can produce light as well. A nebula is a cloud of dust and gas in space. Some nebulas consist of dead or dying stars, while others are areas where new stars are forming. As a result, the gases in these clouds can be similar to those found in stars. These gases can cause the cloud to glow.

■ An exploding star is called a supernova. These stars produce large amounts of light.

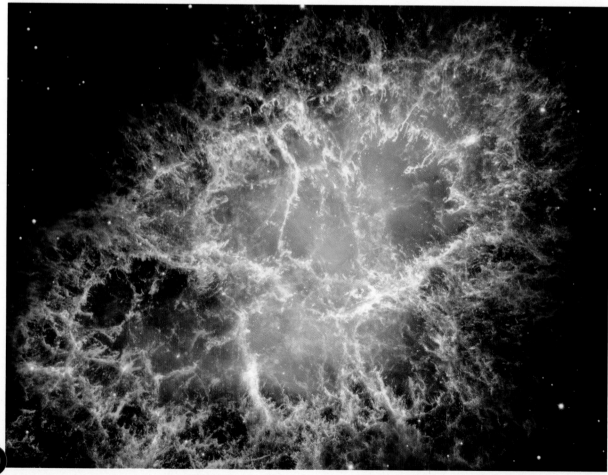

Quasars are the brightest objects in the universe. These starlike objects are about the same size as Earth's **solar system**. Scientists believe they produce as much light as 1,000 galaxies.

The Moon also appears to shine down on Earth. However, the Moon does not create light like the Sun does. Moonlight comes from the Sun. Sunlight hits the Moon and reflects onto Earth. This is how Earth receives most of its light at night.

■ The Moon would not be visible on Earth if the Sun did not shine on it.

Fire

Fire can be a natural or artificial light source. It depends on how the fire is made. People create some fires using tools, such as lighters and matches. Other sources of fire occur naturally, without any involvement from people. These include sunlight and lightning.

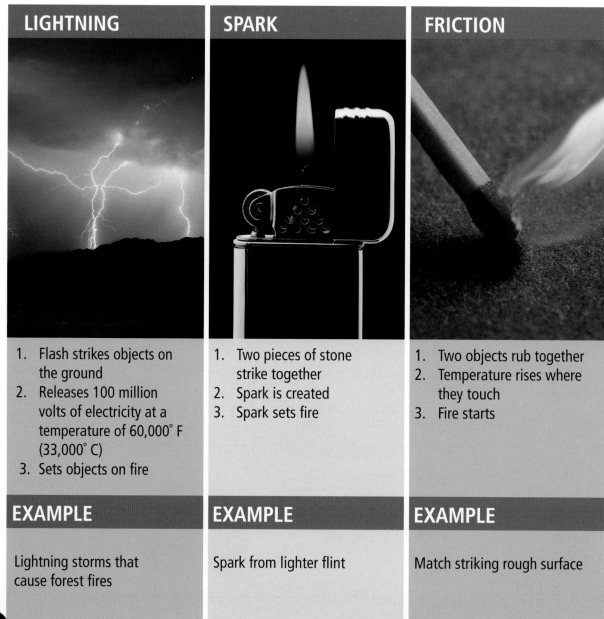

LIGHTNING

1. Flash strikes objects on the ground
2. Releases 100 million volts of electricity at a temperature of 60,000° F (33,000° C)
3. Sets objects on fire

EXAMPLE

Lightning storms that cause forest fires

SPARK

1. Two pieces of stone strike together
2. Spark is created
3. Spark sets fire

EXAMPLE

Spark from lighter flint

FRICTION

1. Two objects rub together
2. Temperature rises where they touch
3. Fire starts

EXAMPLE

Match striking rough surface

Fire is created by a process called **combustion**. Combustion depends on three ingredients. These are oxygen, fuel, and heat. If any of these are missing, a fire cannot start. During combustion, heat removes the water from fuel. This allows the oxygen to touch the fuel. When this happens, the fuel **ignites**, and fire is made. The flames that spring from the fire provide light.

CHEMICAL	SUNLIGHT	EARTH'S CORE

1. Certain chemicals mix together 2. Create a new chemical and heat 3. Heat causes fire	1. Shines through glass lens 2. Lenses concentrate light on one spot 3. Temperature rises at spot 4. Fire starts	1. Temperature is 9,032° F (5,000° C) 2. Heat melts rock near Earth's core 3. Melted rock escapes to surface through cracks 4. Sets fire to nearby objects
EXAMPLE	**EXAMPLE**	**EXAMPLE**
Burning fuel in an automobile engine	Sunshine passing through magnifying glass	Lava from volcanoes

Lightning can travel from cloud to ground and from ground to cloud. It can also move from cloud to cloud.

Lightning

Lightning is a bright flash of electricity that is produced during a thunderstorm. The electricity is created naturally as a result of ice and water within the clouds. It can be very windy inside a cloud. The wind rubs ice particles and raindrops together. This rubbing creates electric sparks.

The electric sparks created in thunderclouds are huge. They leap through the sky as lightning bolts, bringing light to the dark sky. Lightning is so hot that it heats the air, causing it to expand rapidly. This sudden movement of large air masses causes shock waves, which are heard as thunder. Light travels faster than sound, so lightning is seen before it is heard.

A lightning bolt can be up to five times hotter than the surface of the Sun.

LIGHTNING MYTHS

Long ago, people did not know why storms happened. They told stories or myths about storms. Some ancient peoples believed that thunder and lightning were weapons thrown to Earth by angry gods. The Ancient Greeks believed that lightning was caused by a god names Zeus. In Scandinavia, it was believed that thunder came from a god named Thor. The rumbling sound was Thor riding his cart over the clouds.

Electric Light

When people are indoors, they often turn a lamp on to light up the room. The lamp provides light through the use of electricity. Electricity comes from a variety of sources. People have found ways to turn the **energy** in wind, water, and fire into electrical power.

The type of electricity used in homes is called **current electricity**. Current electricity comes from generators. Generators are machines that produce electricity from different energy sources, such as wind, water, coal, and the Sun. Energy from burning fuel turns water into steam. The steam then turns the blades inside the generator. The generator changes **kinetic energy** into electrical energy for people to use.

Electricity moves from generators through large wire cables to houses and businesses. **Electricians** then connect smaller wires in houses to the large wires to bring electrical energy into homes. When a lamp is plugged into a wall outlet or a light switch is turned on, the flow of current electricity creates light.

■ Substations help distribute electricity from the power plant to homes and businesses.

Lighting Technology Through Time

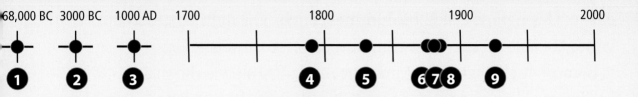

68,000 BC | 3000 BC | 1000 AD | 1700 | 1800 | 1900 | 2000

1 — **2** — **3** — **4** — **5** — **6 7 8** — **9**

1 **About 68,000 BC**
The first lamps are made using fire and a hollow object filled with moss and animal fat.

2 **About 3000 BC**
Candles are invented and used to provide light in houses and outside.

3 **About 1000 AD**
The first street lamps appear in Cordoba, the largest city on the Iberian Peninsula, in southwest Europe.

4 **1792**
William Murdock, a Scottish engineer, experiments with gas lighting and produces the first gas-operated lamp.

5 **1835**
James Bowman Lindsay of Scotland develops an electric bulb lighting system.

6 **1875**
Henry Woodward and Matthew Evans **patent** an electric light bulb.

7 **1879**
Thomas Edison develops the concept for an **incandescent** light bulb.

8 **1880**
Thomas Edison produces a light bulb that can last for 1,500 hours. Previous light bulbs only lasted for 13.5 hours.

9 **1927**
Edmund Germer develops the fluorescent light bulb.

Animal Light

Some plants and animals produce their own light. Chemical compounds within their bodies mix together to create a glowing effect. This light is called **bioluminescence**. The light comes in a variety of colors. The most common color on land is green. This is because it reflects well against green plants. Blue is the main bioluminescent color in the ocean. It reflects well in seawater.

Bioluminescent light is useful to the animals and plants that produce it. Some animals use the light to scare or confuse enemies. At other times, it is used to attract a mate. For some deep-sea creatures, light may simply help them see and find their way around in a pitch-black environment.

■ Bioluminescent fish are only found in ocean environments. Freshwater fish do not have this ability.

What is an Astronomer?

Astronomers are scientists who spend their time studying the sky. They do this to learn more about the universe. Astronomers use telescopes and other instruments to study galaxies, the Moon, planets, stars, and the Sun.

Edwin Hubble was the first astronomer to discover stars outside of Earth's galaxy, the Milky Way. Hubble made other important discoveries about stars and the universe. The Hubble Space Telescope is named after him.

As scientists, astronomers are patient and determined. They often spend years trying to find the answer to a particular problem. Astronomers use their science skills and their ability to use **logic** to solve the mysteries of outer space.

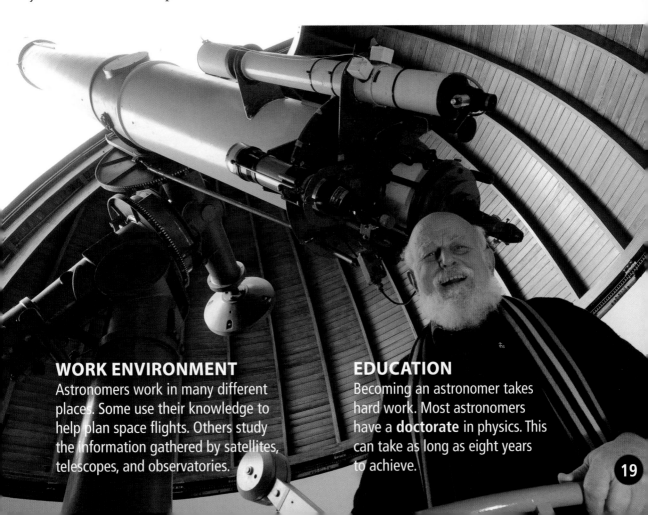

WORK ENVIRONMENT

Astronomers work in many different places. Some use their knowledge to help plan space flights. Others study the information gathered by satellites, telescopes, and observatories.

EDUCATION

Becoming an astronomer takes hard work. Most astronomers have a **doctorate** in physics. This can take as long as eight years to achieve.

Seven Facts About Light Sources

A lightning bolt contains enough electricity to power an average household for two weeks.

In two hours, an average **solar flare** releases enough energy to power the United States for 10,000 years.

A star's brightness is called luminosity.

A flash of lightning between a cloud and the ground can be up to 9 miles (14 km) long.

Cool stars appear red, while the hottest, brightest stars appear blue.

Many forest fires are caused by lightning.

The *aurora borealis*, or northern lights, are caused when solar wind particles hit Earth's **magnetic field**. Solar wind is a stream of particles that is given off by the Sun.

Light Brain Teasers

1 What are the three main categories of natural light sources?

2 How long does it take for sunlight to reach Earth?

3 What is a nebula?

4 Does the Moon produce light?

5 Is fire a natural or artificial light source?

6 Why can lightning be seen before it is heard?

7 What type of electricity is used to power people's homes?

8 What is bioluminescence?

9 Who was Edwin Hubble?

10 What is a star's brightness called?

ANSWERS: 1. Celestial, atmospheric, and terrestrial 2. About 8 minutes 3. A cloud of dust and gas in space 4. No, it reflects light from the Sun. 5. It can be either. 6. Light travels faster than sound. 7. Current electricity 8. Light produced by animals 9. The first astronomer to discover stars outside Earth's galaxy 10. luminosity

21

Science in Action

Light a Bulb

You can create your own electricity. Try this experiment to see if you can make enough electricity to power a light bulb.

Tools Needed

a dark room

a fluorescent light bulb

a comb

Directions

1 Take the light bulb and comb into a dark room.

2 Run the comb through your hair about 20 times.

3 Place the comb on the metal end of the light bulb. Does the light bulb turn on?

4

By rubbing the comb through your hair, you created an electric charge. When the comb touched the bulb, the charge was transferred. The charge then lit the bulb.

Words to Know

artificial: made by human labor

atoms: very small particles

auroras: natural light displays in the sky

bioluminescence: light created by an animal's body

chemical compounds: substances formed when two or more atoms join together

combustion: the chemical process that produces fire and flames

current electricity: electric energy running through wires

doctorate: an advanced university degree

electricians: people who work with electricity or install or repair things that are electric

energy: usable power

fluorescent: able to give off light when exposed to electricity

fuse: join together

galaxies: groups of stars and planets in the universe

halogen: chemical elements that are combined with metals

ignites: sets on fire

incandescent: glowing with a hot bright light

kinetic energy: the energy of movement

logic: the science of getting new and valid information by reasoning from facts already known

magnetic field: the space around a magnetic object in which the magnet has the power to attract other metals

meteors: rocks in space

natural: occurring on its own, not made by humans

nuclear energy: the energy released by a nuclear reaction, such as fusion

patent: to claim the right to be the only person to make, use, or sell a new invention

reflects: turns or throws back light

solar flare: a sudden, short-lived increase of intensity in the light of the Sun

solar system: the Sun and all the planets and celestial bodies that revolve around it

Index

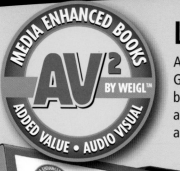

Log on to www.av2books.com

AV² by Weigl brings you media enhanced books that support active learning. Go to www.av2books.com, and enter the special code found on page 2 of this book. You will gain access to enriched and enhanced content that supplements and complements this book. Content includes video, audio, web links, quizzes, a slide show, and activities.

Audio
Listen to sections of the book read aloud.

Video
Watch informative video clips.

Embedded Weblinks
Gain additional information for research.

Try This!
Complete activities and hands-on experiments.

WHAT'S ONLINE?

Try This!	Embedded Weblinks	Video	EXTRA FEATURES
Complete an activity to learn more about a source of light. Learn more about the history of light research with a timeline activity. Write about a day in the life of a researcher who works with light. Test your knowledge of the sources of light with a fact activity.	Learn more about sources of light. Find out more about reactions that create light. Learn more about the science of light.	Watch this video to learn more about sources of light. Watch a video about a technology that uses light.	**Audio** Listen to sections of the book read aloud. **Key Words** Study vocabulary, and complete a matching word activity. **Slide Show** View images and captions, and prepare a presentation **Quizzes** Test your knowledge.

AV² was built to bridge the gap between print and digital. We encourage you to tell us what you like and what you want to see in the future.

Sign up to be an AV² Ambassador at www.av2books.com/ambassador.